From Hunger To Wholeness

Strategies to free yourself from overeating

Caroline Taylor-Thomas
and Pam Kleinot

ACKNOWLEDGMENTS

We have a debt of gratitude firstly to our patients. We appreciate our friends, family, teachers and mentors for all the support they have given us over the years. We want to thank the following people for reading the manuscript and their helpful comments: Dr Sandra Grant, Joscelyn Raven, Agata Pisula, Keith Sylvester, Lindy Goldkorn, Paul Hart, Debbie Cuthbert, Sue Cowan-Jenssen and Katya Orrell. We are grateful to Morris Nitsun for giving us permission to use his illustration on the front cover. Special thanks to Pat Devereaux who has helped us with publishing this book.

First published in the United Kingdom
in February 2018 by Pat Devereaux
on Amazon.Co.UK Books

ISBN-10: 1986864391
ISBN-13: 978-1986864398

CONTENTS

Introduction

WE ARE TWO Psychoanalytic Psychotherapists with experience in treating eating disorders and other forms of substance abuse. In this short book we offer some accessible understandings of the nature of food misuse and also strategies for overcoming this epidemic.

It is our intention to provide you with a roadmap to help understand eating problems and strategies to combat an issue which is blighting so many lives.

While our focus is on destructive patterns of overeating, we believe that the understandings contained here provide a template for other substance abuse as well.

We attempt to marry together psychoanalytic and other understandings of how to stop destructive eating patterns, while addressing the emotional and psychological aspects that drive the problem in the first place.

If you are reading this book it probably means that you have a significant problem with food. You know you have a problem and you have certainly tried countless diets and possibly more extreme measures. You have lost weight and put it on again. You have probably been locked into this revolving door situation for years.

You are either struggling with your food intake, overeating and overweight, or somewhere on the spectrum of obesity.

You feel stuck and always at risk of returning to food as a "solution".

It could mean that you are at risk of serious health problems, both physical and emotional. The misuse of food is threatening to steal your life.

If this is you, you might feel that it is time to bin your previous "solutions" (diets, pills, surgery) and face the real nature of the problem you have.

No one who diets really accepts that they have a problem because every diet contains the same dream — that once the weight comes off it will be possible for you to return to eating as before.

Something has to change if you are going to gain your freedom from a compulsion that inevitably keeps you overweight and unhealthy, physically and emotionally.

We propose a three-pronged approach:

- Strategies to "put out the fire" by stopping the harmful use of food;

- Structures to help contain chaotic eating and;

- To engage with the work of thinking about what makes you overeat in the first place. This will require help usually in some form.

Our aim is to keep this book simple and accessible enough to appeal to young people suffering from this affliction, as well as the ever increasing number of men and women and elderly people who are also struggling with the problem.

We also hope it will be read by families of those affected in order to help them understand the nature and difficulty of what their loved ones are up against.

We recognise that a spectrum is involved, that some people are more seriously affected by this problem than others.

Firstly, a question has to be posed: Do you really want to face the problem that you have, to take responsibility for it, and to commit to addressing that problem. Are you bothered about what is happening to you? If not, read no further.

This problem can be described in several ways: an addiction, something you cannot stop (even when you want to); something that you can stop, but always return to; perhaps an abuse of something you believe gives you pleasure; or a consuming preoccupation with weight and size.

Unconsciously it may represent something deep within that attacks and sabotages the good in you — a form of self-harm.

We believe that abuse of food is as physically and emotionally as damaging as drug addiction and alcoholism or indeed smoking. All substance abuse is about suffering. We believe that people retreat into these substances in order to stave off the pain of living and as a way of numbing unbearable feelings.

Using substances like food has been described as an innocent search for wholeness. The substance is used to make the person feel whole. It is used to cure "the hole in the soul".

However, though these substances are often regarded as "friends", overeating is actually slow suicide, quietly killing off a person both physically and emotionally. The obesity epidemic is claiming lives through serious health problems such as heart disease, cancer, diabetes and strokes, as well as mental health problems such as depression and suicide.

The worst aspect of it is that before this addiction kills you prematurely, it robs you first — it may take away your joy of living, your self-worth, and your relationships.

Obese and seriously overweight people often retreat from the life of relationships and friendship into a world where the most important relationship is the food. Life starts to revolve around the obsession with food, becoming ever more narrow — losing a little weight and then putting on more.

Some practitioners in the addiction field believe that underneath alcoholism and drug addiction lies a primary food addiction. How often have you heard people say that they never had a problem with their weight while they were drinking and smoking?

Overeating becomes addictive and as with any other addiction, you have to put out the fire and stop it before any progress can be made. It is then that the work begins.

Only then will you become present enough in your life to be able to think about the thoughts and feelings driving the problem in the first place, and reflect on what you might want to do to address your problem.

What is food being used for? We believe it is a substitute. Overeating represents a confusion. The really sweet things you are looking for in life cannot be found in a chocolate bar or any other form of sugar. You certainly will not find the sweet things you crave emotionally by overeating. Trying to satisfy your inner hunger by using food in this way only leads to more craving. In order to move forward, it is essential to nail the lie that eating can satisfy you at a deep level.

Anyone can stop abusing food, just like alcoholics and drug addicts can stop abusing drink and drugs or smokers can quit the cigarette. The really tricky bit is to stay stopped.

Even when the abuse of food has been relinquished, it is important to keep working on the self. Remember, if you just give up something, you are still left with the person who used the substance in the first place.

It is necessary to address the underlying issues masked by the abuse of food. The problem is that unless you do some work on thinking and understanding yourself and what drives your food issues, the chances are you will relapse.

You need to be motivated to "put out the fire", and in the following chapter we deal with some of the factors that might motivate you to address the problem at a deeper level. It is important to realise that the seat of the problem is at an unconscious level and the work is about making it conscious so you have a choice to do something about it.

"Out of your vulnerabilities will come your strength"

Sigmund Freud

Chapter 1

Motivation

I T IS POSSIBLE to escape from the grip of an eating disorder and we intend to offer you a roadmap and help in achieving that freedom. We aim to help you understand how you got imprisoned in this state and what you can do about it now.

Something exists inside of you that is on the side of life. This means that there is hope for you, and a life for you beyond the tyranny of food. It is burning inside of you like the light from a candle. That flame can be recognised and encouraged to grow.

We believe that people who abuse food and other substances are desperately trying to find a feeling of wholeness. They do not feel whole in themselves. This is the reason that they turn to food or other substances in the first place.

It is time to find real solutions, creative rather than destructive ways of mending this "hole in the soul."

In the beginning, food is seen as a "friend". It makes those feelings of emptiness and lack go

away and makes things feel better. It works —
for a while at least. Food feels like a tangible
reward, filling that void. Who would want to give
up a solution like that?

Then there is a tipping point and it becomes
the enemy.

The greatest motivation for stopping the
destructive use of food mostly arises when the
painful consequences of using begin to outweigh
the pleasure it brings, on the one hand, and the
pain it allows you to avoid on the other.

There may be other motivations to stop as well,
such as a new job, health problems, a new
relationship, a beach holiday, an important
event you have to attend etc. These motivations
can be temporary or more lasting.

We believe that the hunger for change, and for
a real solution, exists inside you. In the first
instance, it is your relationship with yourself that
will make the difference.

This journey with yourself involves a movement
from self-harm, self-loathing and neglect, to
treating yourself and your body with care, love
and respect. It also involves recognising and
cherishing all the good things that are you.

In physical terms, progress can be amazingly
swift after you have made the decision to stop

the abuse of food: it can vary, but in three days your mind may begin to clear; in three weeks you will be on your way to breaking the dependency and in three months you will probably have gained enough distance to make rational decisions about your food, rather than react to compulsions.

In emotional and psychological terms, change is also possible for you. It will take time to extricate yourself and you will need help, either professional and from family and friends.

It is possible to strengthen the you who is on the side of life through the work of self-reflection. In the process, you will get yourself back as a whole person able to manage real thoughts and feelings.

First, we will take a look at the world that the overeater has become imprisoned by.

"Nothing changes until the pain of using becomes more than the pain of stopping"

A recovering addict

Chapter 2

Retreat To The Food Cave

WE HAVE TO recognise that the Cave-like space created by using food and other substance abuse is a place of comfort and solace from past and present suffering. It is an attractive place, a retreat to the person who has found it, offering a refuge and respite from overwhelming feelings of anxiety and pain, emptiness and hopelessness.

That is the up-side.

However, the price paid for this "solution" is huge and if it persists, the bill goes on getting bigger and can make you emotionally bankrupt.

Overeating involves a state of mind and body where someone gets stripped of a lot that makes them a whole person. It is not only a retreat from life but also represents a loss of a thinking and feeling relationship with the self.

What happens if people lose their capacity to reason? What happens to you then?

The ability to function as a person, with a mental apparatus capable of remembering and reflecting on the self and thinking about consequences is lost or severely impaired.

The person has lost their spark of life and humanity and something deadly has taken over. The part of the personality that is on the side of life has collapsed. The healthy part has been evicted and told it is no longer needed or wanted and all that is left is imprisonment in a choiceless existence.

There is only a hollow shell, alive yet not really living.

Instead of experiencing anxiety and ordinary human thoughts and feelings, overeaters and other substance abusers find another way of managing life. They retreat into the Cave hoping that the substance will make living bearable.

The Cave dweller gets locked into a very primitive and isolated way of being, becoming more and more cut off from themselves and the world around them.

They are lost. They no longer think. Not about the past and how they might have got into this state in the first place, and not about the consequences of what they are doing to themselves or their relationships with others.

The mental apparatus capable of reflecting on what is going on is eroded and leaves a terrible void that has to be filled with something. The person is no longer capable of making good choices for themselves and the void is filled with food or other substances. This has a devastating impact on self-esteem, which also serves to keep you in the substance.

There is no spontaneous reprieve from this state — there is only a downward path to physical and emotional decline. For many, it only ever gets worse.

There is a cycle involved in substance abuse: emotional and physical needs are not met (historically in childhood or in the present); the ability to manage life is depleted and the person does not feel he or she can cope alone; the substance (food or other) is used as a coping mechanism and it works for a while; then the coping mechanism becomes a worse problem in its own right.

Anyone escaping from this vicious cycle is still vulnerable to getting overwhelmed again and reverting to the historic coping mechanism.

Those caught up in this cycle no longer have a choice. They feel completely in the grip of a compulsion over which they have no control. Some may cling to an illusion that they do have control, and they could stop if they really wanted to. However, deep misery exists behind an often smiley exterior.

What do you do when you feel you are in the grip of something over which you have no choice? What can be done to help someone facing such powerful forces within them?

Some will co-exist with the problem and go on using. Some may die early through their using or actually commit suicide because they feel so desperate.

Our experience shows that the only way to regain yourself and your life is to make a decision to say "no"; to see the damage caused by the "solution" and leave the Cave. They attempt to find more creative ways of managing their "hole in the soul".

"I think therefore I am"

Rene Descartes

Chapter 3

Exiting The Cave

Y OU CAN ONLY go on abusing substances if you lose your mind and rid yourself of your capacity to think and know about consequences.

The way out of the Cave involves getting your mind back again.

How do you make contact with that part of the brain that is supposed to look after you when it has been shut down, often for many years? How do you stand up to that part of the brain that tells you it is alright to use one more time — that you do not really have a problem?

Ways need to be found to kick-start the brain, which has sunk into a mindless state: rather like jump-starting an engine that has not been used for some time, or finding new parts for the engine if some are missing.

Exiting the Cave involves a movement from hiding away from human thoughts and feelings, where emotional and physical life is numbed and deadened by the food, to becoming fully alive.

In order to engage with the new life inside you it is necessary to say "no" to the self-abuse. To do this it is necessary to challenge the notion that food gives you what you crave. At best it provides short-term relief but then turns into a bigger problem than the one you had in the first place.

Getting your life back will involve struggle, help and sometimes set-backs. However, over time the aspect of you that is on the side of life will get stronger.

However, it has to be recognised that there is tremendous loss involved — there is no longer food to turn to when things get difficult. There is a long shadow cast when the go-to substance is no longer an option.

The roadmap to new life involves leaving the Cave and opening the door to new emotional territory, feelings that may be turbulent and frightening, but also life-enhancing and loving.

It is not only giving up the substance that is difficult. Very often those wanting to exit the Cave do not like to think about and remember the past, let alone reflect on the present and the future. They are notoriously "touchy" about discussing the issue with others, because they often experience interventions from outside as criticism.

However, the route to new life means becoming involved with yourself and becoming a whole person again. It means reflecting on who you are and where you are coming from, getting to know about this lack of wholeness in you. What was the nature of the hole that the substance filled? If you get to know all about the hole, you may not be so vulnerable to becoming over-whelmed and collapsing into your old "solutions". The seductive appeal of the food "solution" is always there.

The roadmap also involves facing the damage you have done to yourself and all the consequences of your using to yourself and others. When you are using, the consequences often cease to register.

This work not only helps you get yourself back as a whole person, it has a vital role to play in lifting your self-esteem and beginning to fill that hole inside you. It helps in moving to a position where you can accept and love yourself again.

The work also breathes new life into the part of your brain that gives a damn about you and feels you are worth liberating from this system.

"Unexpressed emotions will never die. They are buried alive and will come forth later in uglier ways"

Sigmund Freud

Chapter 4

Psychological Factors

I N THIS BOOK we are not only talking about the weight you carry on your body, we are wanting to involve you in thinking about the weight you carry emotionally in your mind.

Anybody can lose weight, even large amounts of weight, but it is far more difficult to keep the weight off — as anyone reading this book probably knows already.

We believe that in order to maintain a healthy lifestyle it is necessary to try to think about, and hopefully understand, the structure of your particular problem — what made you turn to food, using and misusing it in the first place.

It is important to stress this again: if you just give up something — food, alcohol, drugs, cigarettes — you are still left with the same person who sought solace from this "solution" in the first place.

When you are overweight...Your body is telling a story — is there anyone listening to what it is saying?

If you are a severely overweight person, man or woman, adult or child, your body fat is generally speaking about emotional issues that are being dealt with in the body. In other words, instead of being experienced at an emotional level, feelings are channelled into your body and become lodged there.

So...you don't have any feelings — it is just that your body goes mad.

All behaviour has meaning, and there may be any number of issues underlying food misuse — buried early trauma, neglect, sexual abuse, abandonment, loss and so on. Some of them may be unconscious and hidden. These are very often undigested experiences that are manifested through disordered eating.

The use and abuse of food can serve a variety of functions, but it almost always puts a distance between a person and what they are feeling. Feelings get suppressed by food and you become a stranger from them and your unbearable emotional self — cut off from what is actually going on inside you. It is not only difficult feelings that are lost, good ones go alongside them.

At the same time as feelings get suppressed, people with food problems become more and more preoccupied with food and also more obsessed by it. Everything begins to revolve around food. It is a "solution" that fails.

This can lead to a feeling in others, the people who love you, that you are "absent" in some way — not really with them. And of course that is right — the food eventually takes over and becomes your primary relationship.

This whole serious picture is often complicated by another psychological factor:

DENIAL

People with this problem often cannot think, or face up to the seriousness of their condition.

They will see the statistics on the obesity crisis on television, and shake their heads over what is happening to children in our schools and they may even start another diet— but it does not seem to penetrate and have any real impact on them.

Part of the problem here is that the weighty feelings that are being carried in the body often do not become apparent until the use and abuse of food stops.

Chubby or overweight people are often cheerful and good-natured. See them after they have been "clean" for a while. Often the other side of all that sugar is anger.

When the using stops, people begin to get closer to themselves and their emotions again. This might be difficult and painful, but at least you are re-entering the world and getting yourself back. It is important to remember that they are only feelings. They are not going to kill you and they will pass.

So....what is your body talking about and what weighty feelings are you carrying? The body is talking — are we able to hear? Is anyone listening? Can we think?

<u>Distorted body image</u> and low self-esteem are often the key underlying issues of eating problems, which are compounded by a society obsessed by food, thinness, celebrity, appearance and instant gratification — a quick fix.

Is it something that has previously been too painful to know about, hopefully until now?

We believe the use and abuse of food can serve a variety of functions. It is important to think about what function it serves for you.

What kind of feelings are you or your family member avoiding? This is the real food for thought.

We offer a list:

- Overeating can be a symptom of underlying depression and people often overeat in order to comfort and soothe themselves. Depression may flag up that something is wrong in our lives and in our relationships and that something needs to change. However, if you continue to use food, nothing changes — you just go on using food;

- Food, particularly sugary foods, may represent a substitute for people, a way of avoiding our need for relationships and the really "sweet things" we get from other human beings. Food is always available, but people are not always there when we want them. The food sweetens things up;

- You do not have to feel loss, emptiness, anxiety, anger and the pain of missing someone. You feed yourself. Food does not say no to us, it is always there and available. You are always in control of the food — you can pick it up when you want it and put it down when you do not —until, of course, it gets control of you;

- It can represent a substitute for sex — "better than sex" — and of course retreating into the food is much simpler than the messy business of human relationships. It may also be a way of trying to avoid sexual relationships.

- It may be used to punish. Self-hatred is common in eating disorders, a way of harming the self via the body — in particular, if there are guilty feelings. You may be carrying weight as a badge of shame or guilt — weighty feelings that seem too painful to know about at an emotional level.

- It may be that unconsciously we need to punish ourselves if things are going too well for us — at some level we do not feel that we are deserving of a good life and a healthy body. Something in us may want to spoil our good experiences. What masquerades as a treat actually hurts us.

- People who overeat often numb thoughts and feelings they have and shut down. Instead, they obsess about their next meal and the urgency to gratify their craving for chocolate, cake or whatever the food trigger.

- They get to live in a bubble of putting on weight and taking it off again, then putting it on again. They retreat from life and reality.

"We are only as needy as our unmet needs"

John Bowlby

Chapter 5

Psychoanalytic Understandings

WE THOUGHT IT would be useful to give a brief review of some psychoanalytic theories to help you know you are not alone and make sense of this issue.

We believe that the overeater enters a do-it-yourself feeding world where there is no need for mother, or any other important caregiver, in their lives — he or she lives in a self-sufficient world believing they can provide for themselves, not needing anyone.

They provide themselves with a substitute for the real thing — either because historically there was not an appropriate feeding mother available to them, or where, through no fault of anyone, feeding goes wrong. Thus eating disorders can be seen as an attack on desire and need for something outside of ourselves. Often at the core is a deep feeling of being unlovable.

Put as simply as possible, we are dealing historically with a disturbance at a very early level, between mother/caregiver and child. Later the "solution" that this child, adolescent, adult develops is to find a substitute for the real thing and feed themselves. That could involve food, alcohol, drugs, cigarettes, gambling, sex, shopping.

Comfort eating is not a new concept. Freud considered overeating to be the result of trauma or a significant event in the oral stage of childhood development.

Psychoanalysts, psychiatrists and psychologists have been preoccupied with the subject for a long time and new theories come into play. Psychotherapist Susie Orbach (1978, 1988) argues that fat is not about food, but rather about protection, sex, mother, strength, assertion, anger and love. Her idea was that learning to eat out of stomach hunger rather than mouth hunger meant food could be a pleasure and nourishing when you are hungry rather than something you have a love/hate relationship with.

Psychoanalyst Marilyn Lawrence (1987) says that a woman who is never satisfied with her own body is expressing her despair about her relation to the world. She and her colleagues at the Women's Therapy Centre in London analysed the complex social forces which impact women's relationships with their bodies and came to the conclusion that eating disorders and food-related problems are issues for all women.

"A woman who eats in a compulsive way is actually very bad at asking for appropriate things for herself. She may experience herself as demanding, greedy and insatiable, but she usually ends up doing the nurturing rather than receiving it," she says in chapter co-written with Tamar Selby.

Binge-eating is a form of self-harm. Women's violence and destructiveness is generally aimed at their own bodies, according to psychiatrist and group analyst Estela Welldon (1988).

Psychologist and psychotherapist Anna Motz (2001) suggests that women who harm themselves through overuse of food are trying to say "I hurt". In *The Psychology of Female Violence*, she says that the main type of female aggressive impulse is towards a woman's own body. "The inner sense of emptiness is created and managed through bingeing rather than understanding."

"Give sorrow words; the grief that does not speak knits the o-er wrought heart and bids it break"

William Shakespeare (Macbeth)

Chapter 6

Compulsion

OVEREATERS AND OTHER substance abusers are in the grip of a compulsion to eat, or use other substances, even though they know it is destructive and they want to stop. How is it possible to understand this apparent contradiction?

The answer, we believe, lies in a malfunction in the capacity to move through the losses and grief of early childhood development, beginning with ejection from mother's womb.

Separation and the failure to mourn are central to the understanding of overeating and other substance abuse. Under favourable circumstances, the infant is helped to come to terms with difficulties and grief that emerge as they develop — losses such as having to face the existence of father, who takes mother away, and then the arrival of new babies.

Under less favourable circumstances, these early losses are experienced as traumatic by the baby and may cause an early depression. Everything in his or her world goes bad and everything inside feels bad as well.

In the face of these separations and losses, some babies and later on adolescents and adults, attach to a substitute or symbol, in the form of food, alcohol or drugs, to replace what they really need.

Thus, in infantile terms, thumb sucking and cuddling or a favourite blanket may comfort a child in the absence of the mother or caregiver, representing nourishment and warmth. The child does not have to know feelings about this loss—to mourn the loss of an absent mother/caregiver — he/she finds a substitute in the form of food, alcohol, drugs etc.

During subsequent occasions of loss, this way of managing can become a pattern, a way of coping with life.

Using substances becomes a compulsion and leaves the sufferer in a do-it-yourself world where he satisfies his own needs and is in control of the sources of nourishment.

The substance becomes the anti-depressant, and a way of self-medicating or self-soothing against depression and anxiety. The substance is readily available when those people/important care-givers are not.

After years of avoiding pain by turning to food, the sufferer becomes separated from an internal parent, usually mother, offering proper care and an internal parent, usually father, saying no to the damaging behaviour. This means that there is no aspect of you looking after yourself properly, and no internal figure standing up to the destructiveness.

A backlog of feelings has built up waiting to be faced when the food "solution" is relinquished. This is when the mourning begins. The separation from the food, or whatever substance is being given up, echoes the earliest losses and feelings at this time which may be experienced as overwhelming.

Now that the years of damage caused to the self and others is recognised, the world and everything in it, including the self, may go bad again — as one begins experiencing those earlier losses.

At this stage the overeater is in danger of not only becoming separated from their substance of choice but separated also from any sense of goodness within them or their loving links with the world and the people in it.

Sadly, however, they are not alone. They have a critical and judgmental internal voice to keep them company. The overeater now has to face all the separation and losses he or she has been eating to escape from in the beginning. These have to be worked through or a return to the food is almost inevitable.

The task is to find a caring parent inside of you to feed and nourish you in a healthy way, and another internal parent able to stand up to the destructive behaviour and say, "no, stop it".

*"Feeling real is more than existing; it is finding a way to exist as oneself....
and to have a self into which to retreat for relaxation"*

Donald Winnicott

Chapter 7

A Problem With Self-Soothing

P EOPLE WHO COMFORT/binge eat find it difficult to self-soothe and often resort to managing their stress, anger, anxiety, pain and conflict with food and other substances. Using food in this way is a destructive coping strategy and it is important to find new ways of managing feelings and life experiences.

The ability to self-soothe is linked to early attachment experiences in the first year of life between the baby and primary caregiver (usually the mother). The psychoanalyst John Bowlby (1958, 1969, 1980) observed that children experienced intense distress when separated from their mothers.

The early bond between baby and caregiver is experienced as the main source of safety, comfort and pleasure. As the bond grows the child becomes dependent upon this person to regulate feelings and in the process learns to regulate itself through self-soothing techniques modelled by the caregiver. This becomes the template for future relationships.

If there are insecure attachments, such as if a parent overreacts, ignores the child or does not read the baby's distress signals, then the child's state of mind may not be reflected upon. The child may internalise the parent's fear, anxiety, anger and will not be soothed. This impacts on the person's capacity to self-soothe in later relationships.

The "solution" may be to sweeten things up with food. In this way helplessness and lack of control can seemingly be transformed.

"Feelings of love and gratitude arise directly and spontaneously in the baby in response to the love and care of his mother"

Melanie Klein

Chapter 8

Mothering, Childhood Obesity and Vulnerability

I T IS PAINFUL for any parent to face having an overweight or obese child, with all the feelings of desperation and helplessness that will probably go with it.

You strive to be a good mother, but you face the problem every day. You are certainly not alone.

Up to a third of children aged 2-15 years are overweight or obese in the UK, according to the Royal College of Paediatrics and Child Health (2015).

Another study found that children as young as eight can experience dissatisfaction with the size and shape of their bodies that put them at risk of eating disorders later on.

The World Health Organisation regards childhood obesity as one of the most serious global health challenges for the 21st century.

You do not have to be a perfect parent — just good enough. But good enough mothering, parenting, in this situation is difficult and it involves careful thought·

"In any given moment we have two options: to step forward into growth or to step back into safety"

Abraham Maslow

Chapter 9

The Social Dimension

THE SURGE IN binge-eating and difficulties around food and body, which have plagued women for centuries, take place in a social context. We can all recall the elaborate clothes and headdresses of Elizabeth 1st and Scarlett O'Hara forcing herself into a corset. Today the pressures are so much greater.

Young people and older ones, and more men and boys are under huge pressure to conform to the false ideals of being perfect, and without mess promoted by media and industries geared to making us believe that we can look like the model if only we buy that dress, or suit, or that make-up.

Plastic surgery is one of the great growth industries, with more and more men and women getting their nips and tucks. Eating disorders have also become a growth industry, with dietary aids, therapists and books proliferating.

Even though we are aware of these pressures that we are under, it does not seem to help. At some deep level we seem influenced by the lust to be thinner, prettier, younger.

Even though we know that the healthy way is to accept and love ourselves for who we are and not how we look…but still we go on trying, aspiring for impossible shapes and sizes.

Perhaps the best we can hope for is to avoid the damaging extremes that can be involved with food misuse — anorexia at one end of the scale and obesity at the other. In the meantime, death rates from anorexia are increasing and overeating has reached epidemic proportions.

"We have it in our head that if we fill our stomachs, we'll fill our hearts"

Kate Wicker
(Weightless: Making Peace with Your Body)

Chapter 10

Strategies To Free You From Binge Eating

YOU CAN STOP other substances like drugs, drink and cigarettes but you have to eat —and that is why it is helpful to have a structure around you and your food.

Overeating can be experienced as a DIY "solution" to life. But it moves from a solution and actually becomes the problem in its own right. We propose that you feed yourself what you need and not look for food to comfort you. It is about attempting to deal with difficult and messy feelings rather than avoiding them.

Three aspects are central to this:

- Stop "using" food, particularly sugar and white carbohydrates, in the way that an alcoholic or drug addict uses their drug of choice. Accept that sugar is your drug of choice, your "poison". See it for what it is.

- Turn to someone or something outside of yourself —a therapist, group, friends, family, religion or organisations devoted to addressing this problem (see list of resources at back of this book). No two food addicts are the same, and people have different paths to recovery. However, you do need to establish a relationship with at least one person with whom you can be completely honest about yourself and your food. Many food addicts lack one responsible and reliable adult who they can confide in and who can be there for them in that way.

* Work towards an understanding of why you picked up food in a compulsive way in the first place. This will more than likely involve getting help from that person to think about yourself.

Addicts and alcoholics know that they have to accept that they have crossed a line, and are unable to safely use these substances again. It is the same with people who give up cigarettes. They have to accept that if they pick up one they will descend to the same physical and mental depths they plunged to before they got "clean".

It is the same with sugar — if you have crossed the line, you are like any other addict and there is only one safe route to recovery — abstinence from whatever is your drug of choice.

For some people, one chocolate (or any trigger food) can be the beginning of a slippery slope, first to the illusion of pleasure and then to self-hatred, low self-esteem and shame at not having a say in your life. In order to recover you have to accept that you cannot just have one and it will not matter.

The way forward is simple but not easy:

1. Admit to yourself that you have a serious problem with food, specifically those containing sugar and white flour (name your food of choice).

2. Acknowledge that it is your problem and that you need help with it. It helps to resist blaming other people and making excuses — or even beating yourself up about it.

3. Accept that there is a need for abstinence from sugar and foods containing sugar and white carbs, or whatever your trigger food might be.

Your reward:

By taking these measures you will become healthy rather than overweight and sick. Even better, you will be free of the conflict about what you can and cannot consume.

Remember, when you are using food in an addictive way, only things with sugar taste "good". Once you get past your craving for sugary substances (cravings last between a few days to a couple of weeks), nothing tastes as good as real food.

You will lose weight and your energy will return. You will also find that your motivation grows.

That is the physical reward.

Emotionally the rewards are even greater. You will get your life back. Your zest for life will return, along with your interest in friends, family, culture and sex.

You will become more present in your life and in relationships and will be FREE of the obsession and preoccupation with food. You will turn outwards to other human beings to find what really feeds and sustains you, not inwards. This is real freedom.

If you follow the strategies in this book and commit to thinking about the underlying factors that make you use and abuse food, you will lose weight and achieve a healthy relationship to food.

Strategies— On the side of life:

It is important to be mindful that it is essential to engage in activities that put you on the side of life, rather than involved with the deadly destructiveness of overeating, that will make you lethargic, depressed and send you down a black hole. You will need some strategies to help you with this.

In order to stand up to the part of you that demands instant gratification you have to become aware of what you are doing. You have to think rather than act = eat.

The only way you can go on damaging yourself with food is by not thinking about what you are doing.

It is important to develop discipline around food:

Always have suitable food in your home so that you can eat healthily and not something damaging. Get organised and be prepared.

- Never have food in your home that you are likely to binge on. On most days you may be able to resist that ice cream in the freezer, but the day will come when you probably will eat it. One day you will be able to have trigger foods around you, but it is important to recognise when you are vulnerable. If certain foods "call" to you, get rid of them.

Chaotic eating needs structure

Taking care of yourself is a key factor and move towards a more balanced way of eating. An addiction organisation offers a simple slogan/formula — HALT — to prevent relapse.

H....Are you hungry?
Have you let yourself go too long without proper food?

A....Are you angry?
If you are, is there a way you can deal with it better than tipping into the food?

L....Are you lonely?
Can you call a friend rather than look to food for comfort and company?

T....Are you tired?
Fatigue is a big problem for overeaters — the temptation is to try and get energy through a sugar boost. Can you allow yourself proper time for rest and sleep?

An addition to HALT is thirst (see following section on water)

Three meals a day

Overeaters frequently "graze", consuming huge amounts of calories by eating small quantities of food throughout the day. Three meals a day with nothing in between provides a structure to contain this destructive way of using food.

It involves committing yourself to three reasonably sized meals each day, containing protein, fats, carbohydrates and vegetables. Proper meals will ensure that you get proper nourishment.

The three planned meals each day takes the conflict out of eating and it means that you are not involved in a constant struggle with yourself about what you can have and when you can have it. It also means that if you are careful about timing, you will not have too long to wait between meals.

Trigger foods

Another helpful strategy is to think about your trigger foods — what sorts of foods set you off on a binge?

A "traffic light" system can help with this:

- Red light foods: no go foods such as sugars, chocolates, cakes, ice cream, foods containing white flour. These are your equivalents to alcohol and drugs. You can choose to have these foods, but you need to live with the consequences of what you are doing to yourself. Alcoholics would like to be social drinkers and addicts would like to use recreationally. The successful ones know that in order to remain in recovery, that is not an option for them. So... no sugar and no refined starches, which quickly convert into sugar.

- Amber foods: foods you can have occasionally, like chips and brown bread. You need to be thoughtful about these.

- Green light foods: food you can always have, within reason, such as meat, fish, vegetables, fruit and fats.

It can be helpful to write a detailed food plan for each day and commit yourself to it. Three reasonably sized meals, with nothing in between. Commit the food plan to a friend if that helps.

Patterns of eating

It is important to think about your patterns of eating. People have different triggers. Some people report that sugar or chocolate is not their problem. For others, it may be cereal or salty/savoury foods and even something as apparently healthy as hummus can become a binge food. We are all different and it is about getting to know yourself.

Other apparently "healthy" foods can be problematic as well. Fruit, for example, is fine in moderation, but it is important to see those apples and pears as tiny packets of sugar and they can get abused and tip over into something damaging.

There are also helpful foods to consider. Some people maintain that hot water with lemon and cinnamon tea or porridge helps with cravings for sweet things.

Water

There is mounting evidence that overeaters are often dehydrated — that simple thirst may be confused with the impulse to eat.

Try drinking at least eight glasses, or two litres, of water each day.

When you feel hungry, try having a long glass of water instead of eating. The chances are you were thirsty, not hungry.

In a society dominated by drinking cokes and sodas and teas and coffees, it is amazing how little water we drink.

Exercise

"A sound mind in a healthy body" - **Aristotle**

Exercise puts you in touch with good feelings about yourself. Find something you enjoy such as a brisk walk, the gym, a video, dancing, yoga or pilates. Exercise stimulates those feel-good chemicals in your body and speeds up the metabolism.

Again, it is about doing something good for yourself that is on the side of life. As you walk, you will start to notice the world around you, the wind in your face, the sun on your back. At the gym, you will start bumping into familiar faces. Even alone with an exercise video, you will become aware of your body's gratitude to you as it gets leaner and fitter.

When you exercise the muscles of your body, you are also helping exercise the muscles of your mind. You create a benign circle, speeding up your metabolism and making it less likely to abuse yourself with food. It is all about self-care and being a good parent to yourself.

One of the keys to healing an eating problem is to have a loving and compassionate relationship with yourself.

Weighing In

Weighing in weekly or monthly is your interface with reality. Overweight people often do not weigh themselves because they do not want to know. More frequent weighing can become a problem because you may become obsessed with measuring how you are doing.

Talk to yourself and beware of your critical inner voice.

Yes, that is right — talk to yourself. You will often hear a voice in your mind attacking you — telling you that you are fat, unattractive, too old, unloveable etc.

Try standing up to that voice and even say out loud: "Leave her (him) alone."

And when you are tempted to eat something unhealthy, try saying: "Don't do that to her (him)".

In other words, put a healthy and caring voice between you and the destructive act.

Call a friend

Overeating is an isolating problem. Therefore, if you feel that you are struggling, pick up the phone and call a friend — even if it is the very last thing you want to do. Allow yourself to connect with a person and not food. It is connection with others that changes everything. Honest and trusting relationships can help heal us.

Exceptional days

Do not spoil a family event or a special lunch at a restaurant by being "on a diet". Restrictions can set you up to binge.

Eat a starter, main course and have fruit for desert. Then stop! The problem is that if you do not have the special meal, you may feel deprived, but if you continue to eat you are going to feel that you have "blown it" and you may think that you might as well continue and go for a full-scale binge.

Beware the self-destruct buttons!

These destruct buttons usually come in two forms:

- I have been good for days but I have not lost any weight — so to hell with it, I might as well eat;

OR

- I have eaten badly, so then I may as well continue to eat badly.

Hitting the self-destruct button is a bad idea!

Also remember, "slips" are common in overeating. It is the same with addicts and alcoholics. It is important to forgive yourself, let go and move forward. Beating yourself up about it will only lead you further into the food — perhaps for weeks, months or years. It is a slippery slope!

Have A Survival Plan

As slips can be part of the recovery process, it is important to develop a plan in case you do. Slips can be for a day — but if you do not have a survival plan, they can last for years. If you slip, what will you do, who will you phone?

"One day, in retrospect, the years of struggle are the most beautiful"

Sigmund Freud

Chapter 11

Obstacles, Setbacks And Self-Sabotage

H ERE ARE SEVERAL obstacles to tackling the problem of overeating and obesity. It is generally a long journey with pitfalls along the way. One of the major snags is:

Denial

Denial is a big part of this. People who have this issue often do not really face up to the reality of the problem that they have. They are either genuinely unaware of the seriousness of the problem, or they hide from it, preferring not to think about it.

Plateaux

Plateaux are normal but can cause real problems. A number of people reading this book will want to lose weight for a variety of reasons — health, looks or whatever.

It is important to recognise that at some points of the journey to where you want to be, you will plateau, have setbacks and face obstacles. However hard you try, you stay the same weight or worse yet, you may even put on a little.

If you keep at it you will not stay stuck and you will get where you want to go.

Sabotage

It is important to remember that the impulse to overeat is never far away, even if your food is "clean" and healthy. This fact needs to be recognised and the impulses managed. Addicts and alcoholics often long for a drink or a quick fix. It is alright to have these impulses, but not to act on them. The impulse/craving will pass.

Addicts often go back to their drugs and alcoholics to their drink. Foodies may also slip back into the food. This usually occurs at times of overwhelming anxiety, when other coping mechanisms fail.

It needs to be remembered that you have got an overeater inside you who will not be best pleased with the new regime you have adopted and will be looking to get back in the driving seat and restore the status quo — a nice long party with the sugar, savoury or whatever your binge foods are.

In order to stand up to this aspect of yourself, you need to become aware of the potential around to sabotage yourself. This is where some of the strategies mentioned earlier can be helpful.

It is important to question, for example, whether you are dealing with your anger in an appropriate way — or is it going to deal with you. Are you looking after yourself as you would a friend, or are you neglecting yourself?

Slips

Slips are a big one. Even if you do not consider yourself as an addict, think of it this way. People with a problem of overeating firstly have difficulty getting their eating habits into some kind of balance, and when they do achieve this, it is even harder to maintain that progress. Slips are common and they can go two ways:

- Either you go back into the food for weeks, months or even years.

OR

- You stop immediately, realise it is not the end of the world, and re-commit yourself.

Remember, if you continue, you may have a couple of stones to lose instead of a few of pounds.

Slips are not the end of the world as long as you decide not to make it the end of the world and get into a binge.

Do not beat yourself up. Try and think about what is going on inside you that may have triggered the binge.

You may feel helpless, but go back to your survival plan.

"Whoever does not…give his full consent to the dreadfulness of life, can never take possession of the unutterable abundance and power of our existence; can only walk on its edge, and one day, when the judgement is given, will have been neither alive nor dead"

**Rainer Maria Rilke
(Duino Elegies/Letters 1910-1926)**

Chapter 12

Getting Your Life Back

I T CAN BE extremely challenging to emerge from the psychological retreat offered by food abuse. Perhaps it will be the hardest thing you will ever have to face. It is in the nature of substance abuse that when you stop using, you get in touch with difficult feelings and the impulse is to start using again to suppress and deaden them.

Coming out of the food retreat can involve facing aching despair — a dark night of the soul[1]. Grief and mourning await anyone brave enough to embark on recovery. People have often lost years of their lives, important relationships and opportunities during their abuse. The un-lived life is painful!

Feelings can surge to the surface when people enter the frightening, uncharted territory involved in emerging from abusing food. Feelings often

---

[1] The phrase "dark night of the soul" comes from a poem by St John of the Cross (1542-1591), a Spanish Carmelite monk and mystic, whose *Noche obscura del alma* is translated "The Dark Night of the Soul"

surface with great force and sometimes lead people to relapse back into the "safety" of the food, which is felt to provide a comfort and container for their feelings of anxiety and helplessness.

Addicts of all kinds tend to be recidivists — people who relapse back into their old ways of being. That is why real recovery requires consistency, commitment and hard work.

Getting your eating under control makes you available to start addressing the problems you have and are being covered up and anaesthetised by the compulsive use of food. You begin to realise that you may never find what you are looking for in life, but you certainly will not find it in the food.

If you are on regime, your food tastes better, the cravings diminish and so does the obsession with food. Your relationship with food becomes more ordinary. Remember — the abuse of sugary foods spoil the enjoyment of real food.

Even more important, you begin to become more present in your life, living in the moment, and available to those you love and care about.

There will be messy and turbulent feelings around, but they are feelings that belong to you — they make you more whole, real and present, instead of absent and lost in a sea of obsession and preoccupation. They are the building blocks of your new life, taking you into new emotional territory.

You begin to become alive, rather than using food to blunt your life and stunt yourself emotionally. You become a whole person again.

"It is a joy to be hidden, and disaster not to be found"

Donald Winnicott

Chapter 13

Conclusion

W HEN THE ABUSE of food has been relinquished it is important to keep working on the relationship with yourself, firstly, and then with the world around you. If you just give up something you are still left with the person who used in the first place.

It is necessary to address the underlying issues masked by the food abuse and to realise that it is necessary to go on doing this. The problem is that unless you do some work on thinking and understanding yourself and what drives your food issues, the chances are you will relapse.

Remember it is not true that everything in your life would be good if only you were thin. However, what is true is that while you are using food in a destructive way, you will pay a heavy price emotionally and physically.

It is also true that if you gain an understanding of the problem that you have and its consequences, it tends to spoil your pleasure in using and abusing.

It has been proved over and over that diets do not work. There is evidence that you will actually put on weight. As an overeater/obese person, the only solution is to adopt a safe and healthy way of eating and to care for yourself physically and emotionally. This will almost certainly involve you in giving up sugar and your trigger foods. It will also require a commitment to addressing your emotional issues on an ongoing basis.

Resources

THERE ARE MANY organisations and programmes aimed at helping people with food addictions. The list below is not exhaustive. Helpful resources include:

Beat Eating Disorders – free adult helpline 0808 801 0677
Youthline 0808 8010711
https://www.b-eat.co.uk

Food Addicts Anonymous
https://www.foodaddicts.org/

Help for Men – Men Get Eating Disorders too! (MGEDT)
http://mengetedstoo.co.uk/

Overeaters Anonymous is the food addict's equivalent of Alcoholics Anonymous and Narcotics Anonymous
http://www.oagb.org.uk/

Psychotherapy organisations for a registered therapist:

British Association for Counselling and Psychotherapy (BACP):
http://www.itsgoodtotalk.org.uk/therapists

British Psychoanalytic Council (BPC):
https://www.bpc.org.uk/find-a-therapist

Group Analytic Network (GAN):
http://ganlondon.co.uk/prod/

Institute of Group Analysis:
http://www.groupanalysis.org/FindaTherapist.aspx   (PTO)

(Continued)

United Kingdom Council for Psychotherapy (UKCP):
https://www.psychotherapy.org.uk/find-a-therapist/

Rehabilitation centres

Nightingale Hospital Tel: 020 75357705
https://www.nightingalehospital.co.uk/inpatient-services/

The Priory: Tel: 0800 0773993
http://www.priorygroup.com/eating-disorders

Promis: Tel: 0207 581 8222
https://promis.co.uk/

The Recover Clinic
http://www.therecoverclinic.co.uk/

Bibliography

Bowlby, J. (1958). The Nature of the Child's Tie to his Mother. *International Journal of Psychoanalysis, 39*, 350-371.

Bowlby J. (1969). *Attachment, Vol. 1, Attachment and loss: 2nd edn. London: Hogarth Press; 1982; Harmondsworth: Penguin; 1971*

Bowlby, J. (1988): *A Secure Base: Clinical Applications of Attachment Theory.* London: Routledge.

Brenman, E (2006): *'Separation: A Clinical Problem'* in *Recovery of the Lost Good Object,* Routledge: New Library of Psychoanalysis, New York and East Sussex; first published in the International Journal of Psychoanalysis, 1982

Fairbairn, W. (1952) *Psychoanalytic Studies of the Personality.* London: Routledge

Freud, S. (1917). *Mourning and Melancholia, in On Metapsychology. The Theory of Psychoanalysis,* vol 11, Harmondsworth: Penguin

Freud, S. (1917). Mourning and Melancholia, in *On Metapsychology. The Theory of Psychoanalysis,* Vol 11, Harmondsworth: Penguin

Freud, S. (1920): *'Beyond the pleasure principle',* in Strachey, J. (ed.), The Standard Edition of the Complete Psychological works of Sigmund Freud, vol. 18, (London: Hogarth Press and the Institute of Psychoanalysis).

Klein, M. (1975): *Love, Guilt and Reparation and other works* 1921-1945, London: Hogarth Press and The Institute of Psychoanalysis **(PTO)**

(Continued)

Lawrence, M. (1987): *Fed Up and Hungry: Women, Oppression & Food,* London: Women's Press (UK)

Mitchell, S. (1988): *Relational Concepts in Psychoanalysis: An Integration.* Harvard University Press

Motz, A. (2001) *The Psychology of Female Violence: Crimes Against the Body,* London: Routledge

Orbach, S (1988): *Fat is a Feminist Issue: The self-help guide for compulsive eaters,* London: Arrow Books (first published 1978)

O'Shaunessy, E. (1964): *The Absent Object, published in the Journal of Child Psychotherapy.* Vol 2, Issue 2 (34-43)

Royal College of Paediatrics and Child health, 2015: *https://www.rcpch.ac.uk/obesity*

Steiner, J. (1993): *Psychic Retreats.* London and New York: Routledge

Welldon, E.V. (1992) Mother, Madonna, Whore: The Idealisation and Denigration of Motherhood, New York: The Guildford Press. Originally published, London: Free Association Books

Winnicott D.W. (1971): *Playing and Reality,* London: Pelican

96520877R00049

Made in the USA
Columbia, SC
30 May 2018